Morris Jacob Raphall

Bible View of Slavery

A Discourse Delivered at the Jewish Synagogue

Morris Jacob Raphall

Bible View of Slavery
A Discourse Delivered at the Jewish Synagogue

ISBN/EAN: 9783744732420

Printed in Europe, USA, Canada, Australia, Japan

Cover: Foto ©Lupo / pixelio.de

More available books at **www.hansebooks.com**

BIBLE VIEW OF SLAVERY.

Bible View of Slavery.

A Discourse,

DELIVERED AT THE JEWISH SYNAGOGUE, "BNAI JESHURUM," NEW YORK, ON THE DAY OF THE NATIONAL FAST, JAN. 4, 1861.

BY THE

REV. M. J. RAPHALL, M.A., Ph. Dr.

RABBI PREACHER, AT THE SYNAGOGUE, GREENE STREET, NEW YORK.

NEW YORK:

RUDD & CARLETON, 130 GRAND STREET,

BROOKS BUILDING, COR. OF BROADWAY.

M DCCC LXI.

WHEN the discourse which is now placed before
the public in pamphlet form, was first delivered, I
little anticipated that it would attract and occupy
public attention in the manner and to the extent
which it has done. The subject had not been
chosen by myself; I was called upon to expose a
pernicious fallacy. Under a strong sense of duty I
did it ; not by any reasoning of my own, but by a
statement of facts, supported by the authority of
Scripture. That such a sober statement, and the
inferences to be deduced therefrom, should prove
very unpalatable to men of extreme opinions, and
that they should do their utmost to refute my discourse, was naturally to be expected. Accordingly they have tried their best, from newspaper
paragraphs of a few lines up to elaborate articles
of many columns. With what success, it is for
public opinion to decide. It seems, however, that
the public, like myself, thinks " that facts are facts."
So long as the one great fact is not produced—THE
TEXT OF SCRIPTURE WHICH DIRECTLY OR INDIRECTLY
DENOUNCES SLAVEHOLDING AS A SIN—so long as this
has not been done, my statements remain incontro-
vertible. As that text has not been quoted, which
it never can be, SINCE IT DOES NOT EXIST, all the
fiery attacks and declamations against me are but
" leather and prunella."

It is true that the attempt has been made to find
such a text ; and that Matt. vii. 12 : " All things
whatsoever you would that men should do to you, do

you even so to them," has been quoted. I might answer that this great precept, the practical explication of the command, " Thou shalt love thy neighbour like thyself," was not only known to the ancient Hebrews and even to heathen Greeks, full four hundred years before the sermon on the Mount, but likewise to all Christian nations upwards of 1800 years after that sermon ; but that by ancients and moderns it never was brought to bear on slaveholding till within the last (comparatively) few years. But I prefer to take my answer from the New Testament. The writer of the " Epistle to Philemon" had, before his conversion, been the disciple of Gamaliel, a descendant of that Hebrew sage, who, in the Talmud (tr Sabbath fo. 31), declares that the rule " whatsoever is hateful to thee do not unto others" is the sum and substance of the Law. After his conversion he became one of the principal teachers of Christianity. But though he must have entered into the spirit of the sermon on the Mount far more fully and truly than the writers in the " Tribune" can do—and perhaps for that very reason, he sent back the fugitive slave, Onesimus, to his owner. Proof sufficient on the authority of Paul of Tarsus, that the text, Matt. vii. 12, has no special application to slaveholding.

The long tirade in the " Tribune" of this day must go for what it is worth. It is before the public ; so is my discourse. Each of the two must stand or fall on its own merits. But I am convinced my discourse will not fall, for it embodies "the word of our God, which standeth good for ever.'

M. J. R.

NEW YORK, *Jan.* 15*th*, 1861.

SERMON.

BIBLE VIEW OF SLAVERY.

———◆•◆———

"The people of Nineveh believed in God, proclaimed a fast, and put on sackcloth from the greatest of them even to the least of them. For the matter reached the King of Nineveh, and he arose from his throne, laid aside his robe, covered himself with sackcloth, and seated himself in ashes. And he caused it to be proclaimed and published through Nineveh, by decree of the King and his magnates, saying: Let neither man nor beast, herd nor flock, taste anything; led them not feed nor drink any water. But let man and beast be covered with sackcloth, and cry with all their strength unto God; and let them turn every individual from his evil way and from the violence that is in their hands. Who knoweth but God may turn and relent; yea, turn away from his fierce anger, that we perish not. And God saw their works, that they turned from their evil way: and God relented of the evil which he had said that he would inflict upon them; and he did it not."—Jonah iii. 5–10.

1. MY FRIENDS—We meet here this day under circumstances not unlike those described in my text. Not many weeks ago, on the invitation of the Governor of this State, we joined in thanksgiving for the manifold mercies the Lord had

vouchsafed to bestow upon us during the past
year. But "coming events cast their shadows
before," and our thanks were tinctured by the
foreboding of danger impending over our country.
The evil we then dreaded has now come home to
us. As the cry of the prophet, " Yet forty days
and Nineveh shall be overthrown," alarmed that
people, so the proclamation, "the Union is dis-
solved," has startled the inhabitants of the United
States. The President—the chief officer placed
at the helm to guide the vessel of the commonwealth on its course—stands aghast at the signs
of the times. He sees the black clouds gathering
overhead, he hears the fierce howl of the tornado,
and the hoarse roar of the breakers all around
him. An aged man, his great experience has
taught him that " man's extremity is God's oppor-
tunity;" and conscious of his own inability to
weather the storm without help from on high, he
calls upon every individual "to feel a personal
responsibility towards God," even as the King
of Nineveh desired all persons " to cry unto God
with all their strength "—and it is in compliance

with this call of the Chief Magistrate of these
United States that we, like the many millions of
our fellow-citizens, devote this day to public
prayer and humiliation. The President, more
polished, though less plain-spoken than the King
of Nineveh, does not in direct terms require every
one to turn from his "evil way, and from the
violence that is in their hands." But to me these
two expressions seem in a most signal manner
to describe our difficulty, and to apply to the
actual condition of things both North and South.
The "violence in their hands" is the great
reproach we must address to the sturdy fire-eater
who in the hearing of an indignant world pro-
claims "Cotton is King." King indeed, and a .
most righteous and merciful one, no doubt, in
his own conceit; since he only tars and feathers
the wretches who fall in his power, and whom he
suspects of not being sufficiently loyal and obedi-
ent to his sovereignty. And the "evil of his
ways" is the reproach we must address to the
sleek rhetorician who in the hearing of a God-
fearing world declares "Thought is King." King

indeed, and a most mighty and magnanimous
one—no doubt—in his own conceit; all-powerful
to foment and augment the strife, though power-
less to allay it. Of all the fallacies coined in
the north, the arrogant assertion that "Thought
is King" is the very last with which, at this
present crisis, the patience of a reflecting people
should have been abused. For in fact, the
material greatness of the United States seems
to have completely outgrown the grasp of our
most gifted minds; so that urgent as is our need,
pressing as is the occasion, no man or set of men
have yet come forward capable of rising above
the narrow horizon of sectional influences and
prejudices, and with views enlightened, just, and
beneficent, to embrace the entirety of the Union
and to secure its prosperity and preservation.
No, my friends, "Cotton" is not King, and
"Human thought" is not King. *Adonai Meleck.*
The Lord alone is King! *Umalkootho bakol
mashala,* and His royalty reigneth over all. This
very day of humiliation and of prayer—what is it
but the recognition of His supremacy, the confes-

sion of His power and of our own weakness, the
supplications which our distress addresses to His
mercy? But in order that these supplications
may be graciously received, that His supreme
protection may be vouchsafed unto our Country,
it is necessary that we should begin as the people
of Nineveh did; we must "believe in God."—
And when I say "WE," I do not mean merely us
handful of peaceable Union-loving Hebrews, but
I mean the whole of the people throughout the
United States: the President and his Cabinet,
the President elect and his advisers, the leaders
of public opinion, North and South. If they
truly and honestly desire to save our country, let
them believe in God and in His Holy Word; and
then when the authority of the Constitution is to
be set aside for a higher Law, they will be able
to appeal to the highest Law of all, the revealed
Law and Word of God, which affords its supreme
sanction to the Constitution. There can be no
doubt, my friends, that however much of personal ambition, selfishness, pride, and obstinacy,
there may enter into the present unhappy quarrel

between the two great sections of the Commonwealth—I say it is certain that the origin of the
quarrel itself is the difference of opinion respecting
slave-holding, which the one section denounces
as sinful—aye, as the most heinous of sins—while
the other section upholds it as perfectly lawful.
It is the province of statesmen to examine the
circumstances under which the Constitution of
the United States recognises the legality of slaveholding; and under what circumstances, if any,
it becomes a crime against the law of the land·
But the question whether slave-holding is a sin
before God, is one that belongs to the theologian.
I have been requested by prominent citizens of
other denominations, that I should on this day
examine the Bible view of slavery, as the religious mind of the country requires to be enlightened on the subject.

In compliance with that request, and after
humbly praying that the Father of Truth and of
Mercy may enlighten my mind, and direct my
words for good, I am about to solicit your earnest
attention, my friends, to this serious subject. My

discourse will, I fear, take up more of your time than I am in the habit of exacting from you; but this is a day of penitence, and the having to listen to a long and sober discourse must be accounted as a penitential infliction.

The subject of my investigation falls into three parts :—

First, How far back can we trace the existence of slavery?

Secondly, Is slaveholding condemned as a sin in sacred Scripture?

Thirdly, What was the condition of the slave in Biblical times, and among the Hebrews; and saying with our Father Jacob, "for Thy help, I hope, O Lord!" I proceed to examine the question, how far back can we trace the existence of slavery? .

I. It is generally admitted, that slavery had its origin in war, public or private. The victor having it in his power to take the life of his vanquished enemy, prefers to let him live, and reduces him to bondage. The life he has spared, the body he might have mutilated or destroyed,

become his absolute property. He may dispose
of it in any way he pleases. Such was, and
through a great part of the world still is, the
brutal law of force. When this state of things
first began, it is next to impossible to decide. If
we consult Sacred Scripture, the oldest and most
truthful collection of records now or at any time
in existence, we find the word *Ngebed* " slave,"
which the English version renders " servant,"
first used by Noah, who, in Genesis ix. 25, curses
the descendants of his son Ham, by saying they
should be *Ngebed Ngabadim*, the " meanest of
slaves," or as the English version has it " servant
of servants." The question naturally arises how
came Noah to use the expression? How came
he to know anything of slavery? There existed
not at that time any human being on earth except
Noah and his family of three sons, apparently by
one mother, born free and equal, with their wives
and children. Noah had no slaves. From the
time that he quitted the ark he could have
none. It therefore becomes evident that Noah's
acquaintance with the word slave and the nature

of slavery must date from before the Flood, and existed in his memory only until the crime of Ham called it forth. You and I may regret that in his anger Noah should from beneath the waters of wrath again have fished up the idea and practice of slavery ; but that he did so is a fact which rests on the authority of Scripture. I am therefore justified when tracing slavery as far back as it can be traced, I arrive at the conclusion, that next to the domestic relations of husband and wife, parents and children, the oldest relation of society with which we are acquainted is that of master and slave.

Let us for an instant stop at this curse by Noah with which slavery after the Flood is recalled into existence. Among the many prophecies contained in the Bible and having reference to particular times, persons, and events, there are three singular predictions referring to three distinct races or peoples, which seem to be intended for all times, and accordingly remain in full force to this day. The first of these is the doom of Ham's descendants, the African race,

pronounced upwards of 4,000 years ago. The
second is the character of the descendants of
Ishmael, the Arabs, pronounced nearly 4,000
years ago; and the third and last is the promise
of continued and indestructible nationality pro-
mised to us, Israelites, full 2500 years ago. It
has been said that the knowledge that a particular prophecy exists, helps to work out its ful-
filment, and I am quite willing to allow that
with us, Israelites, such is the fact. The knowledge we have of God's gracious promises renders
us imperishable, even though the greatest and most
powerful nations of the olden time have utterly
perished. It may be doubted whether the fanatic
Arab of the desert ever heard of the prophecy
that he is to be a " wild man, his hand against
every man, and every man's hand against him."
(Gen. xvi. 12.) But you and I, and all men of
ordinary education, know that this prediction at
all times has been, and is now, literally fulfilled,
and that it has never been interrupted. Not
even when the followers of Mahomet rushed
forth to spread his doctrines, the Koran in one

hand and the sword in the other, and when Arab
conquest rendered the fairest portion of the Old
World subject to the empire of their Caliph, did
the descendants of Ishmael renounce their charac-
teristics. Even the boasted civilization of the
present century, and frequent intercourse with
Western travellers, still leave the Arab a wild
man, "his hand against everybody, and every
man's hand against him," a most convincing and
durable proof that the Word of God is true,
and that the prophecies of the Bible were dictated
by the Spirit of the Most High. But though, in
the case of the Arab, it is barely possible that
he may be acquainted with the prediction made
to Hagar, yet we may be sure that the fetish-
serving benighted African has no knowledge of
Noah's prediction; which, however, is nowhere
more fully or more atrociously carried out than
in the native home of the African. Witness the
horrid fact, that the King of Dahomy is, at this
very time, filling a large and deep trench with
human blood, sufficient to float a good-sized
boat; that the victims are innocent men, murdered

to satisfy some freak of what he calls his religion; and that this monstrous and most fiendish act has met with no opposition, either from the pious indignation of Great Britain, or from the zealous humanity of our country.

Now I am well aware that the Biblical critics called Rationalists, who deny the possibility of prophecy, have taken upon themselves to assert, that the prediction of which I have spoken was never uttered by Noah, but was made up many centuries after him by the Hebrew writer of the Bible, in order to smoothe over the extermination of the Canaanites, whose land was conquered by the Israelites. With superhuman knowledge like that of the Rationalists, who claim to sit in judgment on the Word of God, I do not think it worth while to argue. But I would ask you how is it that a prediction, manufactured for a purpose—a fraud in short, and that a most base and unholy one, should nevertheless continue in force, and be carried out during four, or three, or even two thousand years; for a thousand years more or less can here make no difference. Noah,

on the occasion in question, bestows on his son
Shem a spiritual blessing: "Blessed be the Lord,
the God of Shem," and to this day it remains a
fact which cannot be denied, that whatever knowledge of God and of religious truth is possessed
by the human race, has been promulgated by the
descendants of Shem.   Noah bestows on his son
Japheth a blessing, chiefly temporal, but par-
taking also of spiritual good.   " May God enlarge
Japheth, and may he dwell in the tents of Shem,"
and to this day it remains a fact which cannot be
denied, that the descendants of Japheth (Euro-
peans and their offspring) have been enlarged
so that they possess dominion in every part of
the earth; while, at the same time, they share in
that knowledge of religious truth which the
descendants of Shem were the first to promul-
gate.   Noah did not bestow any blessing on his
son Ham, but uttered a bitter curse against his
descendants, and to this day it remains a fact
which cannot be gainsaid that in his own native
home, and generally throughout the world, the
unfortunate negro is indeed the meanest of slaves.

Much has been said respecting the inferiority of his intellectual powers, and that no man of his race has ever inscribed his name on the Pantheon of human excellence, either mental or moral. But this is a subject I will not discuss. I do not attempt to build up a theory, nor yet to defend the moral government of Providence. I state facts; and having done so, I remind you that our own fathers were slaves in Egypt, and afflicted four hundred years; and then I bid you reflect on the words of inspired Isaiah (lv. 8.), " My thoughts are not your thoughts, neither are your ways my ways, saith the Lord."

II. Having thus, on the authority of the sacred Scripture, traced slavery back to the remotest period, I next request your attention to the question, "Is slaveholding condemned as a sin in sacred Scripture?" How this question can at all arise in the mind of any man that has received a religious education, and is acquainted with the history of the Bible, is a phenomenon I cannot explain to myself, and which fifty years ago no man dreamed of. But we live in times when we

must not be surprised at anything.   Last Sunday
an eminent preacher is reported to have declared
from the pulpit, " That the Old Testament requirements served their purpose during the physical
and social development of mankind, and were
rendered no longer necessary now when we were
to be guided by the superior doctrines of the New
in the moral instruction of the race."   I had
always thought that in the "moral instruction of
the race," the requirements of Jewish Scriptures
and Christian Scriptures were identically the same;
that to abstain from murder, theft, adultery, that
"to do justice, to love mercy, and to walk humbly with God," were " requirements" equally
imperative in the one course of instruction as in
the other.   But it appears I was mistaken.   "We
have altered all that now," says this eminent divine,
in happy imitation of Molière's physician, whose
new theory removed the heart from the left side of
the human body to the right.   But when I remember that the "now" refers to a period of which you
all, though no very aged men, witnessed the rise;
when, moreover, I remember that the "WE" the

reverend preacher speaks of, is limited to a few im-
pulsive declaimers, gifted with great zeal, but little
knowledge ; more eloquent than learned ; better
able to excite our passions than to satisfy our
reason ; and when, lastly, I remember the scorn
with which sacred Scripture (Deut. xxxii. 18)
speaks of " newfangled notions, lately sprung up,
which your fathers esteemed not;" when I con-
sider all this, I think you and I had rather continue
to take our " requirements for moral instruction"
from Moses and the Prophets than from the eloquent preacher of Brooklyn. But as that reverend gentleman takes a lead among those who most
loudly and most vehemently denounce slaveholding as a sin, I wished to convince myself whether
he had any Scripture warranty for so doing; and
whether such denunciation was one of those
. " requirements for moral instruction" advanced
by the New Testament. I have accordingly
examined the various books of Christian Scripture, and find that they afford the reverend gentleman and his compeers no authority whatever for
his and their declamations. The New Testament

nowhere, directly or indirectly, condemns slaveholding, which, indeed, is proved by the universal
practice of all Christian nations during many centuries.   Receiving slavery as one of the condi-
tions of society, the New Testament nowhere
interferes with or contradicts the slave code of
Moses; it even preserves a letter written by one
of the most eminent Christian teachers to a slave-
owner on sending back to him his runaway slave.
And when we next refer to the history and
"requirements" of our own sacred Scriptures, we
find that on the most solemn occasion therein
recorded, when God gave the Ten Commandments on Mount Sinai—

> There where His finger scorched, the tablet shone;
> There where His shadow on his people shone
> His glory, shrouded in its garb of fire,
> Himself no eye might see and not expire.

Even on that most solemn and most holy occasion, slaveholding is not only recognised and
sanctioned as an integral part of the social struc-
ture, when it is commanded that the Sabbath of

the Lord is to bring rest to *Ngabdecna ve Ama-
thecha,* " Thy male slave and thy female slave"
(Exod. xx. 10; Deut. v. 14). But the property
in slaves is placed under the same protection as
any other species of lawful property, when it is
said, "Thou shalt not covet thy neighbor's house,
or his field, or his male slave, or his female slave,
or his ox, or his ass, or aught that belongeth to
thy neighbor" (Ibid. xx. 17; v. 21). That the
male slave and female slave here spoken of do
not designate the Hebrew bondman, but the
heathen slave, I shall presently show you. That
the Ten Commandments are the word of God, and
as such, of the very highest authority, is acknow-
ledged by Christians as well as by Jews. I would
therefore ask the reverend gentleman of Brooklyn and his compeers—How dare you, in the
face of the sanction and protection afforded to
slave property in the Ten Commandments—how
dare you denounce slaveholding as a sin? When
you remember that Abraham, Isaac, Jacob, Job
—the men with whom the Almighty conversed,
with whose names he emphatically connects his

own most holy name, and to whom He vouchsafed
to give the character of " perfect, upright, fearing
God and eschewing evil" (Job i. 8)—that all these
men were slaveholders, does it not strike you that
you are guilty of something very little short of
blasphemy? And if you answer me, "Oh, in
their time slaveholding was lawful, but now it has
become a sin," I in my turn ask you, " When
and by what authority you draw the line?" Tell
us the precise time when slaveholding ceased to
be permitted, and became sinful?" When we
remember the mischief which this inventing a new
sin, not known to the Bible, is causing; how it
has exasperated the feelings of the South, and
alarmed the conscience of the North, to a degree
that men who should be brothers are on the point
of embruing their hands in each other's blood,
are we not entitled to ask the reverend preacher of
Brooklyn, " What right have you to insult and
exasperate thousands of God-fearing, law-abiding
citizens, whose moral worth and patriotism, whose
purity of conscience and of life, are fully equal
to your own? What right have you to place

yonder grey-headed philanthropist on a level with
a murderer, or yonder virtuous mother of a family
on a line with an adulteress, or yonder honorable
and honest man in one rank with a thief, and all
this solely because they exercise a right which
your own fathers and progenitors, during many
generations, held and exercised without reproach
or compunction.   You profess to frame your
" moral instruction of the race" according to the
" requirements" of the New Testament—but tell
us where and by whom it was said, " Whosoever
shall say to his neighbor, *Raca* (worthless sinner),
shall be in danger of the council ; but whosoever
shall say, thou fool, shall be in danger of the judgment." My friends, I find, and I am sorry to
find, that I am delivering a pro-slavery discourse.
I am no friend to slavery in the abstract, and
still less friendly to the practical working of slavery.   But I stand here as a teacher in Israel ;
not to place before you my own feelings and
opinions, but to propound to you the word of
God, the Bible view of slavery. With a due
sense of my responsibility, I must state to you

the truth and nothing but the truth, however unpalatable or unpopular that truth may be.

III. It remains for me now to examine what was the condition of the slave in Biblical times and among the Hebrews. And here at once we must distinguish between the Hebrew bondman and the heathen slave. The former could only be reduced to bondage from two causes. If he had committed theft and had not wherewithal to make full restitution, he was "sold for his theft." (Exod. xxii. 3.) Or if he became so miserably poor that he could not sustain life except by begging, he had permission to " sell" or bind himself in servitude. (Levit. xxv. 39 *et seq.*) But in either case his servitude was limited in duration and character. "Six years shall he serve, and in the seventh he shall go out free for nothing" (Exod. xxi. 2). And if even the bondman preferred bondage to freedom, he could not, under any circumstances, be held to servitude longer than the jubilee then next coming. At that period the estate which had originally belonged to his father, or remoter ancestor, reverted to his possession, so that he went forth at once a freeman and a landed proprietor. As his privilege of Hebrew citizen was thus only suspended, and the law, in permitting him to be sold, contemplated his restoration to his full rights, it took care that during his servitude his mind should not be crushed to the abject and cringing condition of a slave. " Ye shall not rule over one another with rigor," is the provision of the law. (Lev. xxv. 46.) Thus he is fenced round with protection against any abuse of power on the part of his employer; and tradition so strictly interpreted the letter of the law in his favor, that it was a common saying of Biblical times and homes, which Maimonides has preserved to us, that " he who buys an Hebrew bondman gets himself a master." Though in servitude, this Hebrew was in nowise exempt from his religious duties. Therefore it is not for him or his that the Ten Commandments stipulated for rest on the Sabbath of the Lord; for his employer could not compel him to work on that day; and if he did work of his own accord, he became guilty of death, like any other

Sabbath-breaker. Neither does the prohibition, thou shalt not covet the property of thy neighbor," apply to him, for he was not the property of his employer. In fact, between the Hebrew bondman and the Southern slave there is no point of resemblance. There were, however, slaves among the Hebrews, whose general condition was analogous to that of their Southern fellow sufferers. That was the heathen slave, who was to be bought " from the heathens that were round about the land of Israel, or from the heathen strangers that sojourned in the land; they should be a possession, to be bequeathed as an inheritance to the owner's children, after his death, for ever" (Levit. xxv. 44–46.) Over these heathen slaves the owner's property was absolute; he could put them to hard labor, to the utmost extent of their physical strength; he could inflict on them any degree of chastisement short of injury to life and limb. If his heathen slave ran away or strayed from home, every Israelite was bound to bring or send him back, as he would have to do with any other portion of his neighbor's

2*

property that had been lost or strayed. (Deut. xxii. 3.)

Now, you may, perhaps, ask me how I can reconcile this statement with the text of Scripture so frequently quoted against the Fugitive Slave Law, "Thou shalt not surrender unto his master the slave who has escaped from his master unto thee" (Deut. xxiii. 16). I answer you that, according to all legists, this text applies to a heathen slave, who, from any foreign country escapes from his master, even though that master be an Hebrew, residing out of the land of Israel. Such a slave—but such a slave only—is to find a permanent asylum in any part of the country he may choose. This interpretation is fully borne out by the words of the precept. The pronoun "thou," is not here used in the same sense as in the Ten Commandments. There it designates every soul in Israel individually; since every one has it in his power, and is in duty bound to obey the commandments. But as the security and protection to be bestowed on the runaway slaves are beyond the power of any individual, and

require the consent and concurrence of the whole
community, the pronoun "thou" here means the
whole of the people, and not one portion in opposition to any other portion of the people. And
as the expression remains the same throughout
the precept, "With thee he shall dwell, even
among ye, in the place he shall choose in one of
thy gates where it liketh him best," it plainly
shows that the whole of the land was open to
him, and the whole of the people were to protect
the fugitive, which could not have been carried
out if it had applied to the slave who escaped
from one tribe into the territory of another. Had
the precept been expounded in any other than its
strictly literal sense, it would have caused great
confusion, since it would have nullified two other
precepts of God's law; that which directs that
"slaves, like lands and houses, were to be inhe-
rited for ever," and that which commands "property, lost or strayed, to be restored to the
owner." Any other interpretation would, moreover, have caused heartburning and strife between
the tribes, for men were as tenacious of their

rights and property in those days as they are now. But no second opinion was ever entertained; the slave who ran away from Dan to Beersheba had to be given up, even as the runaway from South Carolina has to be given up by Massachusetts; whilst the runaway from Edom, or from Syria, found an asylum in the land of Israel, as the runaway slave from Cuba or Brazil would find in New York. Accordingly, Shimei reclaimed and recovered his runaway slaves from Achish, king of Gath, at that time a vassal of Israel (Kings ii. 39, 40). And Saul of Tarsus sent back the runaway slave, Onesimus, unto his owner Philemon. But to surrender to a ruthless, lawless heathen, the wretched slave who had escaped from his cruelty, would have been to give up the fugitive to certain death, or at least to tortures repugnant to the spirit of God's law, the tender care of which protected the bird in its nest, the beast at the plough, and the slave in his degradation. Accordingly, the ex-tradition was not permitted in Palestine any more than it is in Canada. While thus the owner possessed full

right over and security for his property, the exercise of that power was confined within certain
limits which he could not outstep. His female
slave was not to be the tool or castaway toy of
his sensuality, nor could he sell her, but was
bound to "let her go free," "because he had
humbled her" (Deut. xxi. 14). His male slave
was protected against excessive punishment; for
if the master in any way mutilated his slave,
even to knock a single tooth out of his head, the
slave became free (Exod. xxi. 26, 27). And
while thus two of the worst passions of human
nature, lust and cruelty, were kept under due
restraint, the third bad passion, cupidity, was not
permitted free scope; for the law of God secured
to the slave his Sabbaths and days of rest; while
public opinion, which in a country so densely
peopled as Palestine must have been all-powerful,
would not allow any slave-owner to impose
heavier tasks on his slaves, or to feed them worse
than his neighbors did. This, indeed, is the great
distinction which the Bible view of slavery
derives from its divine source. The slave is a

person in whom the dignity of human nature is
to be respected; *he has rights.* Whereas, the
heathen view of slavery which prevailed at Rome,
and which, I am sorry to say, is adopted in the
South, reduces the slave to a *thing*, and a thing
can have no rights. The result to which the
Bible view of slavery leads us, is—1st. That
slavery has existed since the earliest time; 2d.
That slaveholding is no sin, and that slave property is expressly placed under the protection of
the Ten Commandments; 3d. That the slave is a
person, and has rights not conflicting with the
lawful exercise of the rights of his owner. If our
Northern fellow-citizens, content with following
the word of God, would not insist on being
"righteous overmuch," or denouncing "sin"
which the Bible knows not, but which is plainly
taught by the precepts of men—they would
entertain more equity and less ill feeling
towards their Southern brethren. And if our
Southern fellow-citizens would adopt the Bible
view of slavery, and discard that heathen slave
code, which permits a few bad men to indulge in

an abuse of power that throws a stigma and dis-
grace on the whole body of slaveholders—if both
North and South would do what is right, then
" God would see their works and that they turned
from the evil of their ways ;" and in their case, as
in that of the people of Nineveh, would mercifully
avert the impending evil, for with Him alone is
the power to do so. Therefore let us pray.

Almighty and merciful God, we approach Thee
this day, our hearts heavy with the weight of our
sins, our looks downcast under the sense of our
ingratitude, national and individual. Thou, Father
all-bounteous, hast in Thine abundant goodness
plentifully bestowed upon us every good and
every blessing, spiritual, mental, temporal, that in
the present state of the world men can desire.
But we have perverted and abused Thy gifts; in
our arrogance and selfishness we have contrived
to extract poison from Thy most precious boons;
the spiritual have degenerated into unloving self-
righteousness; the mental have rendered us vain-
glorious and conceited; and the temporal have
degraded us into Mammon-worshipping slaves of

avarice. Intoxicated with our prosperity, we
have forgotten Thee; drunken with pride, we reel
on towards the precipice of disunion and ruin.
What hand can stay us if it be not Thine, O God!
Thou who art long-suffering as Thou art almighty,
to Thee we turn in the hour of our utmost need.
Hear us, Father, for on Thee our hopes are fixed.
Help us, Father, for thou alone canst do it.
Punish us not according to our arrogance; afflict
us not according to our deserts. Remove from
our breasts the heart of stone, and from our
minds the obstinacy of self-willed pride. Extend
thy grace unto us, that we may acknowledge our
own transgressions. Open our eyes that we may
behold and renounce the wrong we inflict on our
neighbors. God of justice and of mercy, suffer
not despots to rejoice at our dissensions, nor
tyrants to triumph over our fall. Let them not
point at us the finger of scorn, or say, "Look
there at the fruits of freedom and self-government
—of equal rights and popular sovereignty—strife
without any real cause—destruction without any
sufficient motive." Oh, let not them who trust in

Thee be put to shame, or those who seek Thee be disgraced. Almighty God, extend thy gracious protection to the United States. Pour out over the citizens thereof, and those whom they have elected to be their rulers, the spirit of grace and of supplication, the spirit of wisdom and brotherly love, so that henceforth, even as hitherto, they may know that union is strength, and that it is good and pleasant for brethren to dwell together in unity. And above all things, Lord merciful and gracious, avert the calamity of civil war from our midst. If in Thy supreme wisdom Thou hast decreed that this vast commonwealth, which has risen under Thy protection, and prospered under Thy blessing, shall now be separated, then we beseech Thee let that separation be peaceable; that no human blood may be shed, but that the canopy of Thy peace may still remain spread over all the land. May we address our prayers to Thee, O Lord, at an acceptable time; mayest Thou, O God, in Thy abundant mercy, answer us with the truth of Thy salvation. Amen.

THE END.

BIBLE VIEW OF SLAVERY.

A Discourse,

DELIVERED AT THE JEWISH SYNAGOGUE, "BNAI JESHURUM," NEW YORK, ON
THE DAY OF THE NATIONAL FAST, JAN. 4, 1861.

BY THE

REV. M. J. RAPHALL, M.A., Ph. Dr.

RABBI PREACHER, AT THE SYNAGOGUE, GREENE STREET, NEW YORK.

NEW YORK:

RUDD & CARLETON, 130 GRAND STREET,

BROOKS BUILDING, COR. OF BROADWAY.

M DCCC LXI.

www.ingramcontent.com/pod-product-compliance
Lightning Source LLC
Chambersburg PA
CBHW032135080426
42733CB00008B/1080